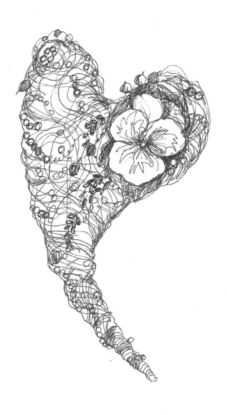

For those people who believe in our ability, and share our dreams

First published in 2002 by Billet doux Design co.
Orchard House, Coney Weston, Bury St Edmunds, Suffolk IP31 1HG Telephone 01359 221421

Floristry: Liz Cowling NDSF FSF and Claire Cowling ICSF MSF Coney Weston, Suffolk. Telephone 01359 221421
Photography - floristry: Peter Griffin, GGS, Norwich, Norfolk Telephone 01603 622500
Photography - landscapes & buildings: Ben Cowling
Sketches: Lizzie Jackson, Bury St Edmunds, Telephone 01284 701406
Design layout: Liz and Ben Cowling together with Colin Barber, Old Newton Graphics, Suffolk. Telephone 01449 675548
Print: Reflex Litho, Thetford, Norfolk. Telephone 01842 754600

A catalogue record for this book is available from the British Library.
ISBN No: 0-9541960-1-5

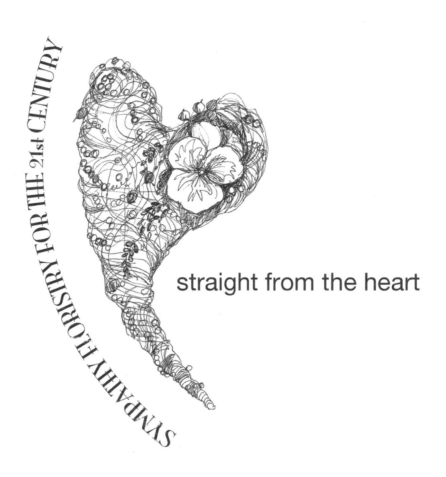

SYMPATHY FLORISTRY FOR THE 21st CENTURY

straight from the heart

Liz Cowling NDSF FSF
Claire Cowling ICSF MSF

If It Must Be...

If it must be
You speak no more with us,
Nor walk no more with us,
Then let us take a patience and a calm,
For even now the green leaf explodes,
Sun lightens stone, and all the river burns.

Anonymous

CONTENTS

8   introduction

12   considerations

18   funeral designs

108 techniques

113 glossary of flower & plant materials

124 bibliography

125 acknowledgments

126 index

introduction

A funeral without flowers is one thing that I cannot imagine... whilst there are many that categorically state that 'flowers are a waste of money' it is important that we understand their necessity, significance and deeper meaning. Throughout history flowers have played an important part in celebrating milestones in life, special occasions and saying that final good bye. Flowers have been given as tokens of love and affection, as well as simply letting friends and relatives know that they are being thought of during a difficult time. They are also appropriate at special anniversaries, birthdays and Christmas, for example, as tokens of remembrance. It is important to let the flowers themselves do the talking, reflecting the character of the person, as well as being relevant to the times in which we live. It is possible to create designs that go further than being just a 'wreath' or 'single ended spray,' designs that are truly memorable. Whilst I wouldn't go as far as saying I believe that sympathy flowers should be fashionable, I do believe that it is possible for them to be 'of the moment' and not staid and stuffy.

I believe that it is vitally important that the designs that we, as professional florists, provide appropriate designs for all of these emotional periods in our lives. It is part of our work to try to dispel the negative thoughts and show customers what is possible without the necessity of gimmicky sundries and miles of polypropylene ribbon. The best and most effective way that we can achieve this objective is by having a comprehensive knowledge of the materials that are suitable for various applications which in turn instils confidence between customer and florist. Arranging flowers for funerals and memorials is as satisfying and creative as any other area of floristry. The possibilities are endless - not always do the tributes have to be expensive, large or formal. Flowers may be transient, but their memory lives on and on...

considerations

considerations

Death is something that touches each and every one of us at some time - family, friends acquaintances. It may be that the death has been expected or totally out of the blue, it may have been through illness or disease, accidental, or occasionally on purpose. The deceased may have been a baby, a child, or an adult. From the florist's point of view the considerations to be made when dealing with the newly bereaved are many and varied. It is important to offer quiet, unhurried advice, whilst ensuring that the suggested tribute's are suitable for the customer's requirements. Establish all the formal details - the day, date, time and place of the funeral. The type of funeral service - traditional, private, woodland burial, cremation etc. There may be religious considerations to be made. The delivery address together with the precise delivery time. It is probable that the customer will volunteer information about the deceased including their age range and character, which is a valuable help to enable appropriate suggestions to be made. Ascertain particular likes and dislikes. Consider the types of flowers that would be most suitable flowers (country, fragrant, classic, exotic etc.). Find out particular colour preferences - pastel, bright, clashing, all white etc., and types of tribute preferred - wreath, spray, cross etc. The style of tribute is equally important whether it should be traditional, trendy, casual or structured. It

may be that there are to be several tributes to be placed on top of the coffin, so ample consideration should be given to this point. Consider the size of the coffin and try to suggest pieces that will not overwhelm the coffin - especially important for children and babies. Big is not necessarily best. Gently suggest a price range. From this basic information it is possible to suggest a whole range of suitable design possibilities within their budget, and enable the florist to create a design perfect for the occasion.

There are hundreds of possibilities regarding the basic shape and design of a tribute. This book will concentrate on some of the more popular, as opposed to the more novel shapes and designs.

It may be wholly appropriate that the flowers are arranged as simple hand tieds, or tiny posies of forget me nots, primroses or violets, each with their own label. Dozens of small posies may be as effective and evocative as one large piece. It may be memorable to reverse the entire process and give guests tiny posies of rosemary or other significant flowers as a token of

appreciation. Tiny posies, are perfect tokens to and from children, whilst a couple of dramatic, choice flowers may be better suited to a younger person. Hand tied bouquets are perfect where flowers are to be sent onward to a nursing home or hospital.

The wreath is one of those tributes that has of late had a rather staid image, but it is really a tribute that has limitless design possibilities as well as being a meaningful tribute and beautiful shape on which to work. The circle signifies never ending love, which is appropriate and wholly apt. The design itself may be traditional, modern, casual, feminine, masculine, rustic, exotic or linked with smaller rings from the children. It may be made on a foam base or constructed entirely from natural materials and include lots of moss, twigs, branches and foliage as well as flower material.

The cross is another tribute that has strong religious meaning, and perfect to be brought up to date by utilising new techniques. Again it may be constructed on a foam frame, or made entirely of natural materials using binding techniques. It is also a shape that is particularly suited to many design possibilities, such as using minimal quantities of flower material, whilst retaining it's original significance. Size is also easily adjusted to be in proportion to the size of the coffin and to the budget.

Posy pads, pillow and cushion shapes lend themselves to being used as bases on which to create part-planted designs which will last for several months. Also excellent for themed pieces of work. These designs may be made on foam bases, wire frames or naturally constructed bases.

With a little bit of thought and lots of imagination stylish and appropriate tributes are easily achievable. Customers never forget the courtesy and consideration shown to them at such emotional times. Flowers are the perfect antidote to soothe and comfort a troubled soul.. florists are the best people to interpret the messages that flowers can convey. The old adage "say it with flowers" is certainly as true today as it ever was.

sympathy
designs

the HEART

straight from the heart -
simple yet distinctive tributes of
massed Gypsophila paniculata
'Million Stars', decorated with a
few choice Helleborus and stems
of China grass. The China grass is
fastened down with steel grass
kisses. The other heart is decorated only with three steel grass
kisses. Suitable for many different age ranges and sizes. Other
alternatives may be to punctuate
the design with Myosotis (forget
me nots), or clusters of berries.

love

everlasting LOVE

19

A rustic cross

made from straight,

shiny lengths of

Bamboo, decorated

with three choice

Arum lilies and

garlanded with

Smilax.

Classic and beautiful Arum lilies
massed together in a cone
shaped framework of grasses.
The design is finished
with a few Marabou feathers -
symbols of a free spirit

21

marguerites

forget me nots

reminiscent of country meadows - marguerites, hellebores and forget me nots in a willow basket. Massed marguerites with the addition of a few strands of steel grass make a charming wreath with panache...

22

marguerit

 23

arum
lilies

arum lilies

timelessly classic - a traditionally beautiful and elegant coffin spray of Arum lilies and Viburnum opulus 'Roseum' enhanced with choice foliage of Eucalyptus, hard Ruscus, Aspidistra elatior and Philodendron. The form of the Arums necessitate the use of strong, unfussy, structured foliage and are best used without many other varieties of flower...

viburnum

opulus

An up to the minute design that's casual and yet full of emotion and feeling. The rather haphazard framework of Typha grass, steel grass and bear grass is a perfect contrast to the clear green spheres of Viburnum opulus 'Roseum.'

Viburnum opulus
Roseum

Clean and simple design,

using flowers of simple form.

Classic and strikingly beautiful...

ites

fragrant
lily of the valley

Posy pad designs that are long-lasting, full of textures and very twenty first century. Straight lengths of Equisetum contrast well with woven China grass, and the edge of reversed leaves of Eleagnus macrophylla. The design is finished off with a delicate bunch of fragrant lily of the valley. Pistachio carnations are densely packed and a single Phalaenopsis orchid nestles on a bed of sisal, two Banksia leaves add a final flourish and yet another texture...

tailiored wreaths with lots of panache for a very special person. Woven Typha leaves form the framework which are then enhanced by the addition of a single choice bloom - Phalaenopsis orchid, Banksia, or Anthurium...

banksia

anthurium

G
Y
P
S
O
P
H
I
L
A

the circle - symbol of never ending love. Simple

Gypsophila paniculata rings are decorated with a

single Phalaenopsis orchid to add sophistication.

Clusters of Viburnum opulus 'Roseum' give a kind

of retro effect. On the facing page the wreath

has been decorated with pansies and forget me

nots - for thoughts and remembrance - and sprigs

of foliage. A length of Smilax draped casually over

the design adds distinction.

PANSIES FOR THOUGHTS

FORGET ME NOTS FOR REMEMBRANCE

POSIES

LOVING THOUGHTS

mixed flower hand tied posies are perfect
to show that you care

♥ 35

lots of different textures combine to make these posy pad designs special as well as long lasting. Candy coloured Ranunculus, sharp green Viburnum opulus 'Roseum' and branches of Larch cones mingle happily together in a casual fashion. Alternatively, concentric circles of flowers, reminiscent of the style favoured by the Victorians, gives a much more ordered appearance. Pistachio carnations, Gypsophila paniculata and Matricaria are used alongside the Ranunculus to give the many different textures.

ranunculus

pistachio

colourful and casually arranged summer flowers in a loose, open heart shaped design. Roses including 'Jacaranda' and 'Mystique,' Dill, Viburnum opulus 'Roseum' and Bupleurum jostle happily with ferns, mixed summer foliage and Hypericum berries. Dozens of roses in rich jewel colours are massed together in the closed heart to make a luxurious tribute...

roses
hellebore
moss

a tight hand tied posy of ruby red roses, complemented by a cluster of lime green
Helleborus foetidus, and enclosed in a moss collar to give texture and
distinction... Gorgeous deep red and golden roses are tightly grouped to one side
of the heart, whilst dark green pads of bun moss cover the other side. Long
tendrils of vine and trails of ivy complete the design.

MOSS
HEARTS
ROSES

41

♥

red roses

for everlasting
LOVE

ivy berries

thinking small -
tiny posies and posy pads, perfect tokens of love and affection from children or for a child. Perfectly scaled down versions of full-sized designs. The posy is massed and grouped whilst the posy pad is delicate, open and loose...

46 ♥

roses
muscari
bupleurum
gypsophila

small posies of lily of the valley, forget me nots, rosemary, pansies, violets or

primroses are poignant individual tokens, or, several may be used as a beautiful

alternative to a traditional tribute strewn across the top of the coffin...

49

CHINA GRASS

THE CROSS

popular for centuries,

woven China grass forms the

base of the cross

which needs few

flowers to complete, yet look

really special. These crosses

are around 18" long and ideal

for small but special tokens

of love and affection.

Delicate choice flowers

add the final touch,

Lily of the Valley, tied

simply with a stem of

China grass, or a rather

abstract group of Muscari...

peace
tranquility

gentle designs, full of meaning, peacefulness and tranquility. The wreath - signifying eternity. - is ordered and has groups of choice flowers in amongst the woodland favourites. In contrast, the posy pad uses lots of nature's treasures - catkins, violets, snowdrops, berries and foliage - which jostle happily together - in a rather casual haphazard fashion.

violets
snowdrops
catkins

a family tribute

with love *sent* *& affection*

happy memories

special tributes for special people ... white coffin spray of choice flowers - roses, Tuberose, Ranunculus, Dill, Molucella and Syringa together with Hypericum, Viburnum opulus 'Roseum' is an ideal family tribute. a pillow that evokes memories of times spent by the sea, using materials that suggest the ambience of the coast is equally suitable. Eringium, shells, hessian, sisal, lichened branches and fresh clean coloured flowers contrast well with the soft grey green of the Eucalyptus and rich dark green bun moss...

a traditional hand tied sheaf of flowers, which includes lots of colour and texture.
Roses, Zantedeshia, Eryngium and Trachelium are complemented by hard Ruscus,
Eucalyptus cinerea and Myrica gale. The cushion is a luxurious tribute massed with
carnations and roses that have been enhanced by the addition of a group of
Hypericum berries, cinnamon bundles and cones for texture, colour and form...

cones
carnations

roses
cinnamon

A posy pad design of a melee of roses in a variation of sizes and colours, within a collar of pine and

Meuhlenbeckia vine which has been decorated with different types of cones and bundles of cinnamon

sticks. Using a similar colour theme the cushion features groups of roses interspersed with carnations,

Achillea, Eryngium and distinctive groups of foliage...

always and forever

roses
roses

roses
roses

simple yet
effective
branches of Larch cones
bound together to make
a symbolic
cross. Long
lasting and
suitable to
be left in
situ for a
long time.

a structured pillow design using lots of nature's treasures. Bamboo shavings together with Muehlenbeckia vine and hay forms the base of the design which has then been decorated with several kinds of cones, cinnamon sticks, pepper berries, Honesty and a single perfect rose. The edges have been neatened with lengths of Typha grass and vine.

country
church

the
cross

A coffin cross in gentle colours is a perfect traditional tribute from the entire

family. This cross features 'Mystique' roses, anemones, Viburnum opulus 'Roseum,

Bupleurum,' Ranunculus, and Ammi majus in pastel colours, which goes well with the

honey coloured wood.

flowers express what words cannot

CATKINS
TUBEROSE
DILL

beautiful pure white flowers combined with cool greens make a design full of
interest and different textures. Ranunculus, anemones, tulips, dill and roses,
provide welcome contrast to the base of foliage, fern and V. opulus 'Roseum.' The
loose wreath features many different flowers - Tuberose, roses, dill, hypericum
berries and spring catkins mingle with several types of foliage.

PURE & SIMPLE

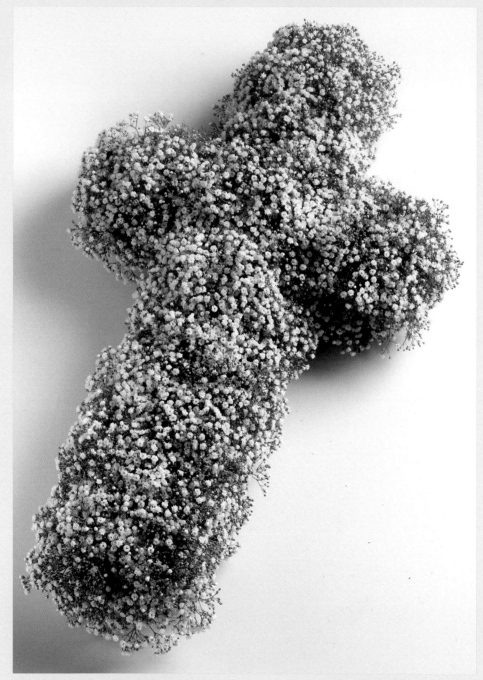

GYPSOPHILA

punctuated with clusters of ivy berries

and decorated with China grass...

SPRING TRUG

SPRING TRUG

SPRING TRUG

SPRING TRUG

SPRING TRUG

SPRING TRUG

WOODLAND

WOODLAND

WOODLAND

WOODLAND

WOODLAND

WOODLAND

serenity

love & affection

remembrance

happy
memories

quiet
thoughts

sunflower
trug

bright, cheerful sunflowers mixed with other summery country garden flowers and lots of dark green foliages in a trug make this arrangement truly memorable. Alternatively the same flowers may be arranged in a more formal way, as in the spray above...

from a summer garden...

bright, cheerful sunflowers arranged casually with summer Calendula, Achillea and a mixture of

foliage make beautiful tributes for young and old... pieces of terracotta and a bundle of Asparagus

form a focal area to the pillow...

Strelitzia regina, banksia and Cymbidium orchids give an exotic feel to this traditional spray. Vibrant colours add to the impact. Similarly, the spray on the facing page has strong forms and colours. Banksia, Cymbidium orchids and roses are complemented by distinctive foliage...

exotic orchids
banksia

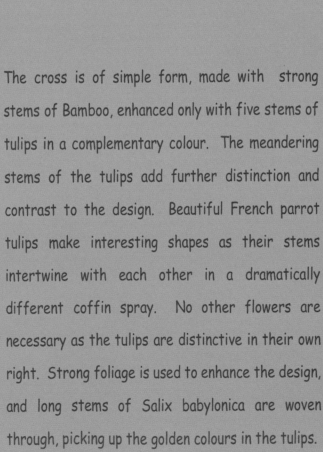

The cross is of simple form, made with strong stems of Bamboo, enhanced only with five stems of tulips in a complementary colour. The meandering stems of the tulips add further distinction and contrast to the design. Beautiful French parrot tulips make interesting shapes as their stems intertwine with each other in a dramatically different coffin spray. No other flowers are necessary as the tulips are distinctive in their own right. Strong foliage is used to enhance the design, and long stems of Salix babylonica are woven through, picking up the golden colours in the tulips.

french tulips

stunningly modern
    clear orange Sandersonia
        are teamed up
    with a pair of Aspidistra elatior leaves
        and tied simply with some lengths
            of Salix babylonica (Weeping Willow)
                to make a distinctive token of
                    love and affection

matricaria

smilax

a tiny willow casket
garlanded with Sandersonia,
Matricaria,
and sharp lime green Smilax

fragile yet beautiful poppies, perfect as a simple token of love and affection arranged casually in a bunch. Slate provides the base for a group of poppies arranged as they may grow amongst Rubus, mosses and Euphorbia. The pillow is based with Bamboo shavings bound securely with wire, decorated with cinnamon sticks, cones, skeletonized leaves and vines. A few intensely coloured poppies add a fragile, ethereal touch to the rather solid base.

poppies
poppies

cinnamon cones

fragility & strength

a strong and solid base of woven willow makes a perfect base on which to entwine beautiful French tulips in vibrant colours. The contrast between the supple stems of the tulips and the sturdy willow adds interest. The other design relies on foliage instead of willow and gives a much less rigid effect...

the
wreath

red roses
for love

rococco

tulips

moss

roses

HEARTS

a modern interpretation of a heart - using layering techniques and emphasis on textures and colour. Translucent Honesty discs, tiny rosebuds and clear blue muscari enhance the base of sisal and foliage. Tiny posies are ideal to decorate small coffins, ensuring that the flowers are in perfect scale...

tiny
tributes
for
babies,
using
delicate
pastel
colours

family tributes

large family tributes using a wide
selection of different flowers -
Euphorbia fulgens, tulips, Eucharis
grandiflora, Matricaria, Lilium longiflorum and roses.

sharp lime green 'Pistachio' carnations are massed together with Viburnum opulus

'Roseum' for an up to the minute heart tribute decorated only with a few strands

of Smilax and a couple of dried Banksia leaves. Similarly, the cross uses sharp

colours for it's distinction - materials include Helleborus, Chrysanthemum santini

'Kermit ' and Viburnum opulus 'Roseum' which have been garlanded with Smilax...

smilax
viburnum
chrysanthemum

96

carnations
BUN MOSS

ELEAGNUS
TULIPS

A few stems of pure white tulips decorate a wreath based with Eleagnus macrophylla. Around the side the grey downy underside of the leaves are uppermost, and on
the top the glossy side is uppermost for variation. Woven China grass and Equisetum
form the base of the posy pad design which is finished with a single stem of Phalaenopsis
orchids. Around the edge of the tribute soft grey Eleagnus provides yet another
contrast in texture and form to the grasses.

CLASSIC arum lilies

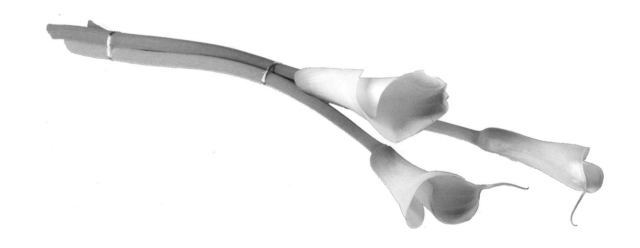

TRADITIONAL
laurel
PHALAENOPSIS

springtime
growing tribute

iris
prunus

iris
prunus

simplicity

rosemary for remembrance

pansies
for
thoughts

christmas
memories

wreaths of rosemary signify remembrance and are particularly

meaningful combined with ivy and a small cluster of pansies - meaning

thoughts. Wreaths of assorted winter greenery - Ilex (holly), ivy, pine,

rosemary, Skimmia japonica and Thuja are ideal as Christmas tributes

that will last for most of the winter.

techniques

BACK TO BASICS

There are several basic techniques that should be observed prior to designing a tribute.

Ensure that all materials, including foliage have been well conditioned. Always cut stems that are to be arranged in foam slantwise to ensure the maximum exposure to the foam. Using a knife gives a cleaner cut. Make sure that the materials chosen are appropriate, that colours and textures are pleasing. Try to ensure that the materials are in proportion and scale - following the general principles of design. Remove any damaged or bruised petals or leaves prior to use. Finish makes all the difference.

Leaves should be cleaned carefully prior to use, leaf shine is not always appropriate, as it gives a somewhat artificial gloss.

Foam frames should be soaked without forcing them under the water, as this tends to create air locks. Chamfering the edges gives a greater surface area on which to work, and generally a more pleasing profile. It is also a good idea to bind two or three times over a frame with narrow pot tape,

minimises the risk of the frame and it's base separating. Frames with rigid bases are preferable for 'planted' designs and any in which some of the foam is to be scooped out ie. to accommodate deep bun moss. When using moss make sure that it is well cleaned, and free of debris such as pine needles or twigs. Cut off some of the back if it is too deep. There are many alternatives to using foam frames other than basing them in the traditional way. Berries, leaves, stems and bark all make interesting base materials. A fine covering of sisal bound with decorative wire and leaves makes a modern base to a tribute. When using sisal and other similar materials, remember that 'less is more.' A more pleasing effect is achieved when it is used sparingly, rather than in big clumps.

When binding materials together use paper covered wire which will give a strong finish that will not cut into the stems. Twist neatly to finish. For decorative binding use sisal bound with bullion or fine coloured reel wire as an alternative to ribbon. Bundle cinnamon sticks neatly together with either paper covered wire or raffia, then mount on a stub wire ready for use.

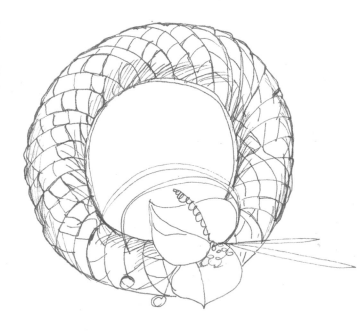

WEAVING

This is a technique that I find very satisfying and relaxing! - as well as looking good, and being an inexpensive way to cover bases. There are numerous materials that are suited to the technique - possibly the easiest is Typha grass as it is really good-tempered. It doesn't bruise easily.

Look at the area to be covered and decide the angle that you'd like the finished weave to be. ie whether the cross-overs are to be at 90° angles or more lazy angles.

Take a couple of leaves and fasten them with dressmaker's pins. Begin the weaving process - going alternately under and over the first leaves. I find it easier to continue from both directions, pinning only now and again until I have completed an area. This allows the leaves to be moved and repositioned slightly if required. When all the frame, or area, has been covered, pin every leaf. Neaten off by fastening a leaf around the side, preferably by gluing. This technique is beautiful in its own right and requires minimal flower material to complete. Hearts and posy pads are possibly some of the easiest shapes to master. Start at the extremities of crosses, finishing off neatly at the centre point.

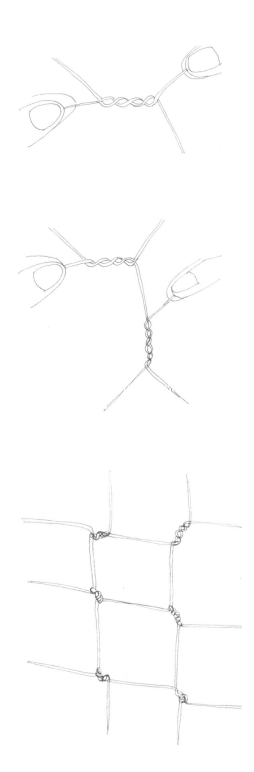

HAND MADE WIRE MESH

For modern designs, hand made wire mesh is extremely useful. May be made with stub wire of various gauges or lengths of fine reel wire, according to the size and density of material to be fixed on to it at a later stage. Whilst the framework needs to be strong it rarely needs to be absolutely rigid, so careful consideration should be made as to the gauge of wire to be used and the size of the 'holes' to be made in the mesh. The technique is useful for using as a shape through which to weave grasses such as Typha, bear grass and steel grass. It is also useful for making coffin covers, which will drape over the coffin and through which flowers and foliage can be woven.

To begin twist two lengths of wire simultaneously. Add further lengths to each end. It does not matter if the mesh is not symmetrical. When the desired size and shape is attained, tidy all the ends, so that they do not snag.

'Tis seen in flowers
And in the morning's pearly dew;
In Earth's green hours,
And in the heaven's eternal blue.

John Clare

glossary

Sympathy floristry is a vast area of our work where I feel that our skills could be far better utilised, both from the artistic and the commercial aspect. It is an area which I feel relies too heavily on sundries and ribbons and not enough on the natural beauty of the materials that we have available to use. One of the most important things of all has to be that the materials are used sensitively to enhance their beauty. Colour is vitally important and similarly the use of form and texture. Often, stems may become an important part of the design. This glossary lists only a small proportion of the materials that we especially love to use whilst creating funeral tributes. There are hundreds more that could be included. Our own personal preferences however, take second place to those of our customer's, but often they are happy to be advised and guided.

ANEMONES

Known as 'Wind flowers' these plants have been cultivated since ancient times and their rich jewel colours and flowers of simple form are perfect for use in funeral designs. The flowers may be used as a hand tied posy

tied with raffia or a decorative string or in more formal pieces. I prefer using them in a casual unstructured way, which seems to suit the flower and allows the beauty of the vibrant petals framed against sooty black stamens to shine through. Available primarily from November through to June.

ANTHURIUM

Originating from the rain forests of Columbia, the

possibilities for this flower are seemingly endless. Long lasting, and in a brilliant range of colours, the only disadvantage is that they easily bruise. The shiny heart shaped (almost plasticy looking) spathe is best used in structured pieces of work where a clean, uncluttered effect is required. Also useful for layering with (dare I say it?) the spadix removed. Keeps best at temperatures around 18°, cut flower food unecessary.

ASPARAGUS ASPARAGOIDES - Smilax

One of my all time favourites. Smilax is just one of those versatile and wonderful materials that is perfect for so many things. It may be quite

expensive, but there is nothing that compares with it to garland pieces of work. The softly coloured leaves complement all kinds of flower material brilliantly. Needs to be kept moist in a cool place - around 5°.

ASPARAGUS SETACEUS

I love using this fern, as a feature in designs that are delicate, kind of dreamy pieces. Although once labelled with a rather stuffy image, this traditional fern is enjoying a revival, and rightly so. One

of those classic examples of being careful about 'how' it's used. Thin out the triangular shaped fronds if too thick for a more feathery effect. Keep in a cool place - minimum 5°. Another equally useful fern that's also enjoying a comeback is Asparagus sprengeri, which is a little more wild looking, but long, curvy and a beautiful clear green. Beware of the spiteful thorns on either type. Available all year.

ASPIDISTRA ELATIOR
Cast iron plant

For decades Aspidistra plants seemed to be labelled as boring and uninteresting, but now the cut foliage seems to be one of those materials that it's difficult to imagine being without. Absolutely ideal for all manner of uses,

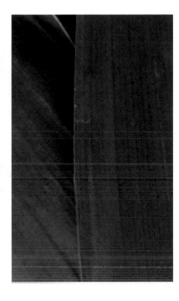

from covering up large areas of foam base (at very reasonable cost), to framing hand tieds, or as a beautiful leaf in large designs, Aspidistra is worth it's weight in gold. Long lasting and available in a variation of sizes, either plain green or variegated. Keep cool - around 5°. Ensure that leaves are perfectly clean, and if desired add leaf shine for an ultra glossy finish.

BAMBOO

The long, tubular stems of Bamboo offer endless pos-

sibilities in funeral work. Ideal for making natural cross shapes that require a minimum of decoration, or bound on to designs for a slightly oriental feel. Most readily available fresh in a bright green colour. Black Bamboo is very beautiful, but very expensive. Needs to be stripped of all foliage for best effect.

CALENDULA - Marigold

These kitchen garden flowers are absolutely ideal for casual, country pieces that also require a vibrant colour scheme. They have been cultivated for many centuries and

evoke a rather masculine, rural cottage charm. Work well with terracotta, and flowers like sunflowers and Solidago. Available throughout the year, although I prefer to use them through the summer months.

CHRYSANTHEMUM FRUTESCENS
Marguerite

Marguerites have to be one of my favourite flowers for lots of designs. I adore their clean, simple shape and their rather romantic country image. I could imagine a coffin

being strewn with stems of Marguerites, and being transported on a farm tumbril by sturdy horses to a tiny country church. More traditional uses could be to use them en masse in a wreath shape or in posies or baskets. Need to be kept simple, or at the most added to other country garden flowers such as Myosotis (forget me nots). Ideal to, or from children. Available most of the year.

CONES

Absolutely perfect for all kinds of uses, and long lasting. Long branches of Larch cones may be bound to form a rustic cross. Individually wired cones make an alternative base material for wreaths or as an additional feature in a design. These may be the

somewhat ordinary Scots pine cones or some of the more unusual, exotic varieties that are readily available from wholesalers. Available in a wide range of sizes, colours and shapes, all year, although they are best used through autumn and winter.

CONVALLARIA
Lily of the Valley

May be considered to be a rather expensive material

to use for funeral tributes, but I believe it to be ideal for a number of reasons. It is absolutely perfect for babies or young children's tributes, where size and scale is vitally important, as well as the tribute being 'memorable and special.' It is lovely just as it is in a simple tied bunch as a token of affection. It is perfect as a flourish on a larger tribute. It is always regarded as special, smells divine and looks wonderful. It's meaning is 'friendship.' Available commercially all year round, outdoor crop available during May.

DENDRANTHEMA
Chrysanthemum

Every florist's standby material. Long lasting, available in a huge range of colours, types and sizes. Personal favourites include the smaller varieties 'Yoko Ono' and 'Stallion' or the wonderful large blooms. Originating from China or Japan, Chrysanthemums are some of those flowers

that always seem enduring and reliable. Often given a rather staid image, they are some of those flowers where the description "it's not what you do but the way that you do it" seems most appropriate. Threaded on to fine wire 'Stallion' look good draped over a formal tribute, or as a sharp solid form in an all green design. Have a distinctive autumnal smell speak autumn and winter, inexpensive, easy to condition and use. Not to be underestimated or written off as passé.

DIANTHUS - Carnations

Another one of those materials that seems to have had a good deal of bad press over the years, but which is so very useful for all kinds of work. Available in a huge range of colours and grades, all year through. Personal favourites include the green varieties 'Pistachio' and

'Prado,' soft pastel pinks and the rich velvety 'Joker.' If using as a basing material, remove the calyx but leave the petals attached, and use German pins to fasten. This method uses less material and gives a much smoother finish. The rather old-fashioned and deliciously fragrant 'Pinks' are ideal for use in summer country garden tributes. Cut between nodes, add cut flower food. Ethylene sensitive.

EUCALYPTUS

A massive family of plant material, used primarily for it's foliage, although some have interesting buds and seed pods that are extremely useful as textures. Ideal as a filler foliage, or for threading and basing. Particular favourites are E. 'Baby

Blue' and E. globulus. Originates from Australia especially New South Wales and Victoria, but now grown extensively across the world. Fragrant and long lasting, many varieties available all year round. E. globulus available during the winter months. Use plain water without any additives.

EUPHORBIA

A large family of plants, of which E. fulgens and E. marginata are the most widely available for com-

mercial use. Graceful arching stems packed full of tiny flowers of simple form. I prefer to remove the foliage as I feel it detracts from the beauty of the flower and the shape of the design, because it has rather a wayward habit. E. fulgens is brilliant for use in large coffin sprays and designs that incorporate loose weaving techniques. E. marginata is useful as a filler. Beware of the milky sap that exudes from the stems as it may be an irritant. Use cut flower food at half strength using lukewarm water (20°).

GYPSOPHILA PANICULATA

Gypsophila has to be one of my current favourites - partly because it has often been labelled as 'naff' and therefore it becomes a bit of a challenge to make it look good! and partly because I think it is very much a flowerl 'of the moment' and perfect for ' retro style' design

work, and also because it is relatively inexpensive. It is really one of those materials that can make a statement or can look just like a bunch of flowers with a bit of gyp. I find 'Million Stars' much the easiest to use, it tends to be stronger in the stem and the flowers are nice and compact. Use cut flower food. Available all year round.

HEDERA

Wild tree ivy, trailing lengths of variegated ivy, single large leaves, strong stately stems of Hedera erecta, ivy root - all have a major place in funeral floristry. Perfect for a wide range of uses, basing, in textured work and as a filler. Long lasting, in a wide range of shapes and

sizes. Clusters of berries may be used as a design feature in their own right. Ensure that leaves are clean, treat with leaf shine if desired. Ivy root is ideal for texture in pillows and rustic designs. Also ideal for inclusion in Christmas wreaths. Foliage available throughout the year. Berries available through the winter months.

HELIANTHUS ANNUS
Sunflowers

These beautiful flowers are now available in such a wide range of wonderful colours and sizes that it is an absolute pleasure to use them and work with their happy faces. I love them arranged casually in trugs, or as feature flowers in

designs. They are also excellent tied simply with raffia or decorative string. The centres of the flower are useful as a texture, used recessed deep down. I prefer to remove the foliage, as this is often damaged and bruised. Sunflowers originate from the Americas. Available most of the year, although at their best during the summer months. Condition carefully using cut flower food. Perfect for young people.

HELLEBORUS

I like to use many different kinds of Hellebore. I love their simple form,

their shape, and their wonderful variations in colour. I like to use H. foetidus in abundance - as a filler and as a focal flower. Their intense lime green colour enhances all kinds of other materials and is 'of the moment.' Works especially well with Marguerites, Myosotis, roses, Viburnum opulus ' Roseum.' The traditional Christmas rose- H. niger are exquisitely beautiful, yet frighteningly expensive flowers, that are not often used commercially. H. orientalis in their antique shades, reminiscent of days gone by, are stunning to use in special designs.

HYACINTH

Fragrant flowers in a wide range of colours. Very useful for natural 'growing style' designs or hand tieds. May be used en masse to good effect or with other spring flowers - Tete a tete, tulips, narcissi, etc. Do not recut the stems, leave as supplied. Use cut flower food for bulbs. Originate

from Western Asia, now cultivated extensively in Holland for the cut flower trade. Available from October through to May.

HYPERICUM

Beautiful ovate berries that are absolutely perfect as an additional

texture in all kinds of designs. Available in a wide range of colours and sizes from soft yellowy-apricot to rich conker brown. Favourites include 'Honey Flair,' and 'Excellent Flair.' Available all year round. Flower food unnecessary, does not appear to last as well in metal buckets and containers.

LICHENED BRANCHES

Those people who are fortunate enough to have a readily available supply of lichened branches to use

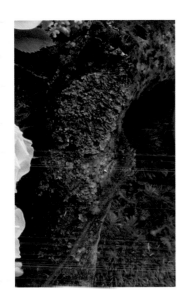

are indeed lucky. They are especially useful as design features in anything that suggests 'seascape. or woodland' Gives strenth to a design.

LONGIFLORUM LILIES

Originating from Japan, the flower is extremely popular and used exten-

sively. Not a particular favourite of mine but one with a valued place in sympathy and funeral designs, and also a good cut flower for church arrangements . Lovely used in a classic sheaf, with the addition of choice foliage or as a full length coffin spray. Individual flowers useful in design work. Purchase when the buds still closed but showing colour. Safest to remove the stamens as the pollen can stain clothing, although I feel that this detracts from the beauty of the flower. Use cut flower food at half strength. Available all year round.

MISCANTHUS SINENSIS VARIEGATUS
China Grass

China grass is a beautiful grass in a soft variegated green and cream. It is one of those special materials from which it is possible to conjure up a design with that looks really special and with lots of impact, at little cost and not too

much effort. Perfect for weaving and using as a natural tie for hand tied designs. Available all year round, average 35-40cms in length. Long-lasting, keep in a cool place, around 5°.

MOSS

So versatile and useful in hundreds of ways. Bun moss is beautiful for covering large areas quickly, and gives an area of quiet to a design. Sometimes requires the back trimming off, so that it is not so deep. Sometimes, it may be helpful to scoop out some of the foam base

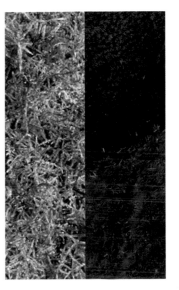

that is being worked on. Flat moss is ideal for using to make a casual base covering for woodland themed pieces, made into shapes (such as small hearts or spheres bound with bullion). Tillandsia is perfect for using sparingly in woven designs, or as a base on which to nestle a choice bloom. Reindeer moss is often useful when a particular texture is required. Keep in a cool place, make sure that all twigs and debris is removed prior to use for optimum effect. Available all year through.

 119

MYOSOTIS
Forget me nots

These have to be one of my most favourite flowers as a token of esteem and affection. Incurable romantic that I may be! - I realise that they are not the most practical of flowers to use, but the connotations surrounding

them and the simple, bright blue flowers mean that they are well worth the care required to maintain them in optimum condition. Best used in simple hand tied posies, or as a filler flower within delicate loose wreaths. Also beautiful to hand to guests after the service, or to place inside the coffin. Available from spring through to mid-summer. Condition carefully, using cut flower food.

ORCHIDS

There are so many kinds of orchids that are wonderful

to use in funeral designs - Phalaenopsis, Paphiopedilum, Cymbidium, Dendrobium and Vanda. All add a touch of luxury and opulence to a design, and do not necessarily have to be used in abundance to create the required effect. Also extremely useful are Vanda roots, these are a wonderful colour and pliable, so brilliant to thread over and through work. Available all year, condition well, using cut flower food. Sensitive to ethylene and low temperatures.

PANSY

Literally meaning thoughts, pansies are an ideal flower to use if a little flower folk lore is felt to be in order. Teamed with a few sprigs of Rosemarinus officiale is a perfect little token bunch. The old fashioned Heartsease is a pretty little flower which is lovely used in 'planted' posy pad designs along with other cottage garden flowers, foliage and branches. The larger flowers with the

smiling face - need to be well conditioned, after which they make a lovely addition to casual, loose wreaths.

PAPAVER - Poppy

Not a flower widely used for funeral floristry, however I like the fragile, almost ethereal quality that the flower has, their clear vibrant colours, the distinctive stem and

somewhat erratic way that the buds open. I like to use them, especially in designs where the stems are visible and can become an additional design feature. They always appear to me to be a 'young' kind of flower, so especially appropriate for young people's tributes or, simple tied bunches. Not long lasting, but nonetheless beautiful.

PRIMROSE

Another flower of simple form which can be used effectively made into tiny posies strewn all over the coffin. If desired a tiny individual label can be attached to each to identify the sender. Perfect if

the request is for flowers and donations. May also be used as plants in 'growing' posy pads for lasting tributes.

RANUNCULUS

Originating from the eastern Mediterranean,

these have to be one of my favourite flowers. Simple shaped flowers made up of dozens of fine papery looking petals, in a wonderful selection of colours, ranging from pure white to majestic purple, pale pink to magenta, vibrant lemon, bicolour. Mmmm. Absolutely wonderful for using in all types of designs - casual, textured, posies. Available nearly all year, use cut flower food.

ROSES

Has to be the Queen of all flowers. Red the classic flower of love, yellow for friendship, white for purity and spiritual love. Commercially grown roses are available in so many types that it would be possible to write a whole series of books on favourites and uses. From a single stem to a tribute made entirely of roses, the message is still the same. That it's for someone special. For tributes to (or from) babies and children,

I particularly like the tiny Italian roses. Larger pieces tend to need larger headed varieties - some favourites are 'Jacaranda' 'Ecstasy' & 'Vendella.' Also good to use are the 'hips' or any discarded roses that have had the petals removed. The stamens are usually a wonderful colour and add an extra dimension and texture. Condition carefully remove the lower leaves, cut slantwise with a sharp knife. Use flower food.

ROSMARINUS OFFICINALIS
Rosemary

Aromatic herb that signifies 'remembrance' and 'constancy in love.' The soft grey foliage is lovely as a filler in hand tieds or as a base material for a

more formal tribute. Avoid using the new spring growths as it may have a tendency to wilt quickly. Available most of the year.

♥ 121

SANDERSONIA
Chinese Lantern Lily

One of New Zealand's leading cut flowers, and a beautiful flower to use for lots of different styles. Good in hand tieds - arranged simply, or threaded individually - to

garland a small casket for example. Clear and bright colour. Sensitive to ethylene.

TULIPS

Another one of those flowers that has so many

uses in floristry. Particular favourites are the 'parrot' varieties and French tulips with their long pliable stems. Ideal for hand tieds - used en masse or in formal work. Good also as a flower where the stems may be used as a design feature. Although available all year, best used through the winter and spring.

TYPHA LATIFOLIA
Reed Mace

Long, strap like leaves which are ideal for a wide number of design ideas.

Woven areas make design features that are quick and easy with lots of style. Typha is ideal to loop around casual designs, perfect to bind round hand tieds as an alternative to ribbon. Dries off nicely, which is an added bonus.

VIBURNUM

The Viburnums are a really useful group of shrubs that are good for a number of uses. Viburnum opulus 'Roseum' with it's sharp green snowball heads is distinctive and useful in

large scale pieces. V. opulus 'Compactum' has heavy clusters of beautiful glossy red berries and are good to use as a feature in design work throughout the autumn and early winter. Viburnum tinus - a kind of old fashioned shrub - may be used as a filler foliage and is also good for padding out sheaf style hand tieds. May be purchased plain, when in flower, or berried, according to season. The ovoid berries are a wonderful blue/black colour.

VINES & CLIMBERS

There are many various kinds of vine that are invaluable for design work. These range from Clematis to Wisteria. Honeysuckle and Jasmine are also useful. They may be bound round a piece of work or

added as loops. Muehlenbeckia either fresh, or dried is good to 'bed' materials down on.

ZANTEDESCHIA
Calla

Elegant funnel shaped flowers of simple form, with lots of style. Originating from South Africa, the flower is now widely cultivated. Available in an

enormous range of sizes and an ever increasing array of colours. The classic white Arum is perfect used on it's own, in traditional pieces such as a coffin spray, sheaf or classic; large arrangements. It is the traditional Easter lily. The smaller coloured varieties are perfect for design work, and their beautiful, pliable stems are perfect for looping around work. Available most of the year. Prefer to be conditioned in shallow water containing flower food and an optimum 8 to 15°.

HARD MATERIALS

There are many other materials that are particularly useful for utilising in our work. Shells, and Eryngium and succulents

such as Echeveria and Aeonium may be appropriate in pieces with a seaside theme. Slate, terracotta and stone may be useful for country, rustic style posy pads. Branches, bark and wood shavings are also useful, especially Silver Birch bark.

BINDING, BEDDING & TYING

Sisal, coconut fibre, linen watten, raffia and pieces of leather are all useful for adding texture into

designs or bedding down choice flowers in minimalist pieces. A band of sisal is good for tying simple hand tied bunches, as is linen watten. Raffia is appropriate for use in rustic country style work, however I often feel that too much is used, and prefer it used sparingly. Bullion, coloured reel wires and paper covered wires are useful for tying, binding together or adding strings of berries.

BIBLIOGRAPHY
The Royal Horticultural Society Gardeners Encyclopaedia Plants & Flowers 1991
Flower Council of Holland - 2001
Foliage for Florists - Veronika Strong 1996
Decorative Cut Flowers - Coen Gelein & Nees Joore 1988

USEFUL ORGANISATIONS
The Society of Floristry
0870 2410432
The Society of Floristry is a non profit making organisation dedicated to raising the standards of professional floristry. Examinations, judges and examiners training courses.

PROFESSIONAL WORKSHOPS
Innovative commercial floristry for the twenty first century...
Liz & Claire Cowling 01359 221421 & 01359 221628

acknowledgements

I seems only a few days ago that we were awaiting the publication of our first book - Straight from the Heart - bridal floristry for the twenty first century. The feelings of excitement, anticipation and nervousness were similar to the very first times that we entered floristry competitions. Why are we doing this? Will we make complete and utter fools of ourselves? Will anyone like our designs or appreciate our views? Over the years we have made some spectacular faux pas in amongst our successes. Some things have remained consistent however, our love of experimenting with new techniques, watching other designers create floristry with love and respect, and seeing customers delight in our work. We never expected that the interest in our published work would result in another title being produced so quickly. The compilation has been a real family affair, Claire - my youngest daughter - and myself, the floristry and text, together with Ben, my youngest son, the page layout (with direction from you know who!). The excitement this time around has not only been with producing the floristry and text, but with seeing each page come to life as a young man of 14 grows in confidence daily, as his skills at the computer increase. It has been an absolute pleasure to work with two of my children who are also two of my best friends. Not only now do I have to contend with getting the floristry right but also the layout to the very last pixel!!! Well done, both of you. Thanks to Lizzie Jackson for the sketches, Nick Armstrong for the loan of coffins, a big thank you to Jane Lambert for proof reading and to Colin Barber, for his advice and skill. Thanks too to all at Reflex Litho for another brilliant print job. Finally, to Mum and the rest of the family - thanks for putting up with all the weeks of muddle... 'til the next time!

INDEX

Achillea 59,72,73,74
Ammi majus 38,53,54,63,64,65,92
Anemone 63,64,68,114
Anthurium 31,114
Arums 20, 21,25,100,123
Asparagus 75
Asparagus asparagoides 20, 27, 33,48,81,94,95,114
Asparagus setaceus 41,74,92,114
Asparagus sprengeri 114
Aspidistra elatior 21,25,53,73,76,77,79,80,92,100,115
Aucuba japonica variegata 75

Bamboo 20,61,78,115
Banksia 29, 31,76,77,94
Barley 71
BASKET 22,68,69,72
Bear grass 21,68,72,73
Berries 38,44,45,54,57,65,67,72,73,74,83,103
BINDING TECHNIQUE 60,78
Bird of paradise 76
Bun moss 41,55
Bupleurum 38,46,47,63

Calendula 75,115
Calla 56,123
Carnations 29,37,55,57,59,73,94,95,96,97
Catkins 53,65
CHAPLET 101
CHILDREN'S PIECES 22, 32, 33,35,46,48,49,66,81,90,91
China grass 19, 22, 28, 29,47,50,51,67,90,101,119
Chinese lantern lily 80,81,122
CHRISTMAS WREATH 105
Chrysanthemum 95,116
Chrysanthemum frutescens 22, 23, 27,115
Chrysanthemum parthenium 35,37,81,92
Cinnamon 57,58,61,83
Clematis 85,123
COFFIN CROSS 63
COFFIN SPRAY 25,54,86,92
Cones 36,53,57,58,60,61,83,87,116
CONSIDERATIONS 12
Convallaria 28,48,49,50,51,71,91,116
Courgettes 75
CROSS 14, 20,50,60,63,66,67,78,95
CUSHION 57,59
Cymbidium 76,77,120

Dendranthema95,116
Dianthus 29,37,55,57,59,73,94,95,96,97,116
Dill 38,53,54,63,64,65,92

Eleagnus macrophylla 28, 29,90,98,99
Eryngium 55,56,59,92
Equisetum 28,99
Eucalyptus 25,56,59,72,79, 85,92,117
Eucharist 92
Euonymus 73,74,75
Euphorbia fulgens 53,68,69,92,117

FAMILY TRIBUTES 54,63,92
Feathers 21
Flat moss 40,75,82,89,102
Forget me nots 22, 33,35,48,49,120
French tulip 78,79,84,85,122

Gaggle 56
Galanthus 53
Galax 69,75,87,101
GARLAND 81
Grape hyacinth 46,47,90
GROWING POSY PAD 102
Guelder rose 25,26,32,35,36,53,54,61,63,64,65,68,74,85,86,87,91,94,95,97
Gypsophila paniculata19, 32, 33,37,46,47,66,67,117

HAND MADE MESH 21, 26
HAND TIEDS 13, 21, 26,34,35,46,56,80,88,100,103
Hard Ruscus 25,75,
Hay 61,83,
HEART 18,38,39,41,43,90,94,96,97
Hebe 69
Hedera 21, 25,41,44,45,55,59,67,69,71,83,86,87,88,89,97,102,103,104,105,117
Helianthus 72,73,74,75,118
Helleborus 19, 22, 27,40,69,95,118
Hessian 55
Holly 105
Honesty 61,83,90
Hyacinth 34,53,68,118
Hypericum 38,54,57,65,72,73,74,118

Iris 103

Ivy 21, 25,41,44,45,55,59,67,69,71,86,87,88,89,97,102,104,105

Jasminum officiale 102

Larch cones 36,53,60,87,
Laurel 101
Lichen twigs 55,69,89,119
Lilac 54
Lily 92,119
Lily of the valley 28,48,49,50,51,71,91,116
Longiflorum lily 92,119
Lunaria annua 61,83,90,

Mahonia 83
Marabou feathers 21
Marigold 75,115
Marguerites 22, 23, 27,115
Matricaria 35,37,81,92,
Miscanthus sinensis variegatus19, 22, 28, 29,47,50,51,67,90,101,119
Mollucella 54
Moss 40,41,55,75,82,89,102,119
Muehlenbeckia 58,75,123
Muscari 46,47,90,
Myosotis 22, 33,35,48,49,120
Myrica gale 56

Orchids 29,53,76,77,99,101,120

Pansy 33,48,49,71,102,120
Papaver 82,83,120
Pepper berries 61
Phalaenopsis 29, 30, 32,53,99,101,120
Philodendron 25,79,100,
Phormium tenax 53,68,74,76,87,
Physalis 83,
PILLOWS 15,55,61,75,83,
Poppy 82,83,120
Primrose 71,102,121
Prunus 92,103
POSY 34,40,46,48,49,71,88,91,
POSY PADS 15, 28, 29,36,37,53,58,64,69,99,102

Ranunculus 34,35,36,37,38,53,54,64,68,91,97,121
Reed mace 21, 26, 28, 30, 31,53,61,85,87,96,122
Rose 38,39,40,42,43,46,47,54,55,56,57,58,59,61,63,64,65,69, 72,73,74,76,77, 86,87, 89,90,92,97,121
Rosemarinus officiale 22,35,48,104,105,104,105,121
Rosemary 22,35,48,121
Rubus 75,82,86
Ruscus 25,56,59,

Salix babylonica79,80,
Sandersonia
Senecio 23, 33
SHEAF 56,100,
Shell 55
SINGLE ENDED SPRAY 73
Sisal 29,90,103
Skeletonized leaves 83
Skimmia japonica 55 76 77
Slate 82
Smilax 20, 22, 27, 33,48,81,94,95,114
Snakegrass 28,99,
Snowdrops 53
SPRAY 25,73,76,77,79,86,92,
Steel grass 19, 23,76,77,
Strelitzia 76
String 55
Sunflower 72,73,74,75,118
Syringa 54

TAKING ORDERS 12
Tete a tete 102
Terracotta 75
TEXTURED DESIGN 55,57,59,83,94,96,97,
TOKEN 48,71,
Trachelium 56,
TRUG 68,72,
Tuberosa 54,65,
Tulip 34,55,63,64,68,69,78,79,84,85,88,92,98,102,12
Typha latifolia

Viburnum opulus 'Roseum' 25, 26, 32,35,36,53,54,61,63,64,65,68,74,85,86,87,91,94,95,97,122
Viburnum tinus 53,63,68,122
Vine 61,74,75,83,123
Violet 49,53,

WEAVING 28, 29, 30, 31,50,51,96,99,
Willow 79,80,84,
WREATH 14, 27, 30, 31, 32, 33,44,45,53,65,74,84,85,87,98,104,105

Xanthorrhoea australis 19, 23,76,77,
Xerophyllum tenax 21,26,68,72,73,

Zantedeschia 20, 21, 25,56,100,123